The

C000053529

by Iain Gray

Lang**Syne**

PUBLISHING

WRITING *to* REMEMBER

WRITING *to* REMEMBER

Strathclyde Business Centre
120 Carstairs Street, Glasgow G40 4JD
Tel: 0141 554 9944 Fax: 0141 554 9955
E-mail: info@scottish-memories.co.uk
www.langsyneshop.co.uk

Design by Roy Boyd
Printed by Thomson Litho, East Kilbride
© Lang Syne Publishers Ltd 2005
ISBN 1-85217-112-X

The Hunters

The Hunters

MOTTO:
I accomplish the hunt.

CREST:
A greyhound.

TERRITORY:
North Ayrshire.

Chapter one:

Origins of the clan system

by Rennie McOwan

The original Scottish clans of the Highlands and the great families of the Lowlands and Borders were gatherings of families, relatives, allies and neighbours for mutual protection against rivals or invaders.

Scotland experienced invasion from the Vikings, the Romans and English armies from the south.

The Norman invasion of what is now England also had an influence on land-holding in Scotland. Some of these invaders stayed on and in time became 'Scottish'.

The word clan derives from the Gaelic language term 'clann', meaning children, and it was first used many centuries ago as communities were formed around tribal lands in glens and mountain fastnesses.

The format of clans changed over the centuries, but at its best the chief and his family held the land on behalf of all, like trustees, and the ordinary clansmen and women believed they had a blood relationship with the founder of their clan.

There were two way duties and obligations.

An inadequate chief could be deposed and replaced by someone of greater ability.

Clan people had an immense pride in race. Their relationship with the chief was like adult children to a father and they had a real dignity.

The concept of clanship is very old and a more feudal notion of authority gradually crept in.

Pictland, for instance, was divided into seven principalities ruled by feudal leaders who were the strongest and most charismatic leaders of their particular groups.

By the sixth century the 'British' king

doms of Strathclyde, Lothian and Celtic Dalriada (Argyll) had emerged and Scotland, as one nation, began to take shape in the time of King Kenneth MacAlpin.

Some chiefs claimed descent from ancient kings which may not have been accurate in every case.

By the twelfth and thirteenth centuries the clans and families were more strongly brought under the central control of Scottish monarchs.

Lands were awarded and administered more and more under royal favour, yet the power of the area clan chiefs was still very great.

The long wars to ensure Scotland's independence against the expansionist ideas of English monarchs extended the influence of some clans and reduced the lands of others.

Those who supported Scotland's greatest king, Robert the Bruce, were awarded the territories of the families who had opposed his claim to the Scottish throne.

In the Scottish Borders country - the notorious Debatable Lands - the great families built up a ferocious reputation for providing warlike men accustomed to raiding into England and occasionally fighting one another.

Chiefs had the power to dispense justice and to confiscate lands and clan warfare produced a society where martial virtues - courage, hardiness, tenacity - were greatly admired.

Gradually the relationship between the clans and the Crown became strained as Scottish monarchs became more orientated to life in the Lowlands and, on occasion, towards England.

The Highland clans spoke a different language, Gaelic, whereas the language of Lowland Scotland and the court was Scots and in more modern times, English.

Highlanders dressed differently, had different customs, and their wild mountain land sometimes seemed almost foreign to people living in the Lowlands.

"The spirit of the clan means much to thousands of people"

It must be emphasised that Gaelic culture was very rich and story-telling, poetry, piping, the clarsach (harp) and other music all flourished and were greatly respected.

Highland culture was different from other parts of Scotland but it was not inferior or less sophisticated.

Central Government, whether in London or Edinburgh, sometimes saw the Gaelic clans as a challenge to their authority and some sent expeditions into the Highlands and west to crush the power of the Lords of the Isles.

Nevertheless, when the eighteenth century Jacobite Risings came along the cause of the Stuarts was mainly supported by Highland clans.

The word Jacobite comes from the Latin for James - Jacobus. The Jacobites wanted to restore the exiled Stuarts to the throne of Britain.

The monarchies of Scotland and England became one in 1603 when King James

VI of Scotland (1st of England) gained the English throne after Queen Elizabeth died.

The Union of Parliaments of Scotland and England, the Treaty of Union, took place in 1707.

Some Highland clans, of course, and Lowland families opposed the Jacobites and supported the incoming Hanoverians.

After the Jacobite cause finally went down at Culloden in 1746 a kind of ethnic cleansing took place. The power of the chiefs was curtailed. Tartan and the pipes were banned in law.

Many emigrated, some because they wanted to, some because they were evicted by force. In addition, many Highlanders left for the cities of the south to seek work.

Many of the clan lands became home to sheep and deer shooting estates.

But the warlike traditions of the clans and the great Lowland and Border families lived on, with their descendants fighting bravely for freedom in two world wars.

Remember the men from whence you came, says the Gaelic proverb, and to that could be added the role of many heroic women.

The spirit of the clan, of having roots, whether Highland or Lowland, means much to thousands of people.

Chapter two:

Royal huntsmen

In an age of supermarkets and convenience foods, it's easy to forget that to put fresh meat on the table centuries ago required the skills of hunters trained in the art of tracking down and killing game.

Royal palates demanded a regular supply of game, ranging from wild boar to deer, and vast acres of parkland and forest throughout Europe were, in effect, royal larders.

The huntsmen appointed to protect these hunting preserves became important members of the royal household and even adopted 'Venator', the Latin form for their profession of hunter, as their surname.

The name later took the English form of 'Hunter.'

A family known as Venator served as hunstmen to the Dukes of Normandy, in France, and following the Norman Conquest of

England in 1066 they settled in England.

The Hunters did not fight at the side of William the Conqueror at the battle of Hastings, but followed him later to England.

The wife of one of the descendants of the Hunters who later settled in Scotland was a lady-in-waiting to William the Conqueror's spouse, and is thought to have been one of the ladies who worked on the famous Bayeux Tapestry.

This linen strip, 223ft long and 1.5ft wide, graphically depicts the events leading up to the Battle of Hastings and the actual battle itself.

By the late eleventh to early twelfth century the Hunters had found a new home in Scotland and, close on 1,000 years later, are still to be found on the land in the north of Ayrshire where they first settled.

A Willieme le Venator, or William the Hunter, had by 1116 built a timber stronghold on the land that would later take the name of Hunterston, or 'Hunters-town', in Ayrshire, and by the middle of the thirteenth century this had been replaced with a much stronger structure built from stone.

It is believed that the Pele Tower, which survives to this day, was constructed around this time.

The exact date is not known, but from an early period after their arrival in Ayrshire the Hunters were appointed Royal Huntsmen.

What the historical record does show is that by the fifteenth century they were the hereditary keepers of the royal forests of the west coast islands of Arran and the Little Cumbrae.

The Hunters were among the many Ayrshire lairds who repelled the threat of Norse invasion at the battle of Largs in 1263, first entering the historical record as defenders of Scotland's freedom.

King Hakon of Norway had sailed with a mighty fleet from Bergen in July of 1263 in response to a warning that Scotland's Alexander III was determined to enforce his

The Battle of Largs

claim to the Hebrides.

Hakon's fierce Viking raiders plundered Bute, Islay, and Kintyre before sailing to lie off the west coast township of Largs.

Alexander III hastily assembled a force of militia raised through the efforts of local lairds such as the Hunters and placed them on hills above the beach to meet the threat of mainland invasion.

A violent storm blew many of Hakon's vessels onto the beach and, in an attempt to recover precious cargo from these ships, many of the Norsemen ventured ashore.

They were met by the militia, however, and after a series of violent skirmishes were driven back to those vessels that were still seaworthy. Hakon died only a few weeks later at Kirkwall, in Orkney.

Scotland had been saved from Norse invasion, thanks, in no small part, to the martial ardour of Ayrshire lairds such as Hunter and their retainers, and the battle is commemorated annually at Largs when a Viking long ship is ceremoniously burned.

The name of Aylmer le Hunter is to be found on the infamous parchment known as the Ragman Roll, on which Scottish lairds and magnates were compelled to sign a humiliating treaty of fealty to Edward I, Hammer of the Scots, in 1296.

Signed by 1,500 bishops, earls, and burgesses such as Hunter, the parchment is known as the Ragman Roll because of the profusion of ribbons that dangle from the seals of the signatories.

Signing a treaty of fealty is one thing, but honouring its terms is another. In common with many others who had not had any option but sign the treaty, the lairds of Hunterston avenged this insult to their honour by supporting the cause of their nation in the bitter Wars of Independence, that ravaged late 13th and early 14th century Scotland.

The climax of the Wars of Independence was the battle of Bannockburn, fought near Stirling in the summer of 1314, but many of the earlier key incidents took place on the Ayrshire lands known so well to both the great freedom fighter William Wallace and the warrior king Robert the Bruce.

Proof of the Hunter family's loyalty to the cause of Scotland's freedom comes in the form of a curious charter for the lands of Ardneil, dated May 2, 1374, and signed by Robert II.

Still in the possession of the Hunters of Hunterston, the charter confirms the grant of land to William Hunter, as reward for the rendering of faithful service.

A condition of retaining the lands is that the reigning monarch must be paid a silver penny in rent, at Hunterston, on the Feast of Pentecost, also known as Whitsun, or the seventh Sunday after Easter.

Successive lairds of Hunterston, up until the present day, have kept a collection of silver pennies in the off chance that the reigning king or queen actually decides to drop in to claim the rent!

Chapter three:

Battle honours

While dedicated to the care of both their own Ayrshire lands and the royal forests, the Hunters continued to serve their nation on the battlefield – often at fatal cost to themselves.

John, the 14th Laird of Hunterston, fell with his king, James IV, at the disastrous battle of Flodden on September 9, 1513, while Mungo, the 16th Laird, fell 34 years later, at the battle of Pinkie, near Musselburgh, on the east coast of Scotland.

The defeat for the Scots at Pinkie was part of what was known as the Rough Wooing – an attempt by England's Henry VIII to force agreement for the proposed marriage of his son, Edward, to the infant Mary, Queen of Scots.

Over the succeeding centuries the Hunters would continue to serve their country on the battlefield. Robert, a grandson of the 20th Laird of Hunterston, served with distinction both as a soldier and a diplomat.

During the War of the Spanish Succession, in which Britain was engaged in war with France, he served under the Duke of Marlborough, the commander of the British forces in the Netherlands, taking part in the famed actions at Blenheim, in 1704, Ramillies, in 1706, Oudenarde, in 1708, and Malplaquex, in 1709.

Hanging up his sword and spurs, he later served as British governor of Virginia and later of New York.

During the Indian Mutiny, Gould Hunter-Weston, husband of Jane Hunter-Weston, the 26th Laird of Hunterston, was present at the recovery of the British residency at Lucknow in September of 1857 after Indian soldiers and civilians who had revolted against British rule had seized it.

His son, Lieutenant-General Sir Aylmer Gould Hunter-Weston, became the 27th Laird of Hunterston following the death of his mother in 1911.

During both the campaign to win the Sudan back from Egypt that culminated in the battle of Omdurman in 1898 and the Boer Wars of 1899 to 1902, he served on the staff of Kitchener, while he was divisional officer to Sir John French, commander of the British Expeditionary Force in France from 1914 to 1915.

In charge of the British Army's VIII Corps, he also played a leading role in the ill-fated Dardanelles Campaign, a bloody exercise in attrition that dragged on throughout most of 1915 to January 1916.

The disastrous campaign involved a brave but futile attempt by British, French, and Dominion forces to seize the Turkish Dardanelles Strait that connected the Aegean with the Sea of Marmara, in the hope it would knock Turkey out of the war.

Troop landings were made on the Gallipoli peninsula in April of 1915, but between December of that year and January of the following year they had to be withdrawn, after more than 250,000 casualties had been sustained.

The debacle forced future Second World War Prime Minister Winston Churchill from his post as First Lord of the Admiralty.

Following Gallipoli, Hunter-Weston later commanded VIII Corps on the Western Front, and after the war was the recipient of many honours, including that of the Distinguished Service Order.

A Conservative and Unionist Member of Parliament for North Ayrshire and Bute from 1916 until 1935, he was responsible for commissioning the architect Sir Robert Lorimer to restore Hunterston Castle, north west of West Kilbride, on the Ayrshire coast.

Sir Aylmer died in a fall from a turret in his ancestral home in March of 1940.

The restored castle, which still has its original roof beams, is adjacent to Hunterston House, work on which began in 1799, and which was extended in 1835.

The Hunters of Hunterston lost a legal battle against a Compulsory Purchase Order in 1956 by the then South of Scotland Electricity Board for land at Hunterston to build a nuclear power station.

Located two miles north of West Kilbride, on the coast, the Hunterston 'A' power station opened in 1964, while the Hunterston 'B' station was commissioned in 1976. When completed, the Hunterston 'A' station was at the time the biggest nuclear plant in the world.

Despite these encroachments on their land, however, the Hunters of Hunterston are unique in that they are among the few ancient Scottish families to still live on the site of where they first settled.

The Clan Hunter Association, with branches around the world, was founded in 1970, and Madam Pauline Hunter of Hunterston and of that Ilk, became 30th Laird and Clan Chief following the death of her father, Neil, in 1994.

Her father had not only continued a Hunter tradition of skill in archery, but was also a highly skilled sailor, representing Britain in two Olympic games and winning a silver medal.

Chapter four:

Medical honours

Two brothers who were descended from the Hunters of Hunterston gained lasting fame for their separate contributions to the world of medical science.

Born at Long Calderwood, East Kilbride, in 1718, William Hunter proved to be something of a child prodigy, for at the tender age of 13 he entered Glasgow University with the aim of studying for a career in the Church.

Finding he did not possess the necessary religious calling, however, he studied medicine at Edinburgh University. He moved to London in 1741, and by the time of his death in 1783 he had become internationally renowned as a medical teacher, writer, and anatomist.

Recognised as having played a key role in removing obstetrics from the hitherto exclusive domain of midwives, he established obstetrics as a branch of medicine – attending Queen Charlotte, wife of George III, at the birth of her children.

He bequeathed his vast collection of anatomical, zoological, botanical, and geological specimens to Glasgow University for display in a museum, in addition to a valuable collection of paintings, manuscripts, books, and coins.

Known as the Hunterian Collection, they are now housed and available for public view at numerous locations within the university.

William's younger brother, John, born in 1728, also gained lasting fame in the world of medical science as the founder of pathological anatomy and of a rigorous scientific approach to surgery – once famously declaring it was his aim to prevent surgeons from acting like "armed savages."

Although he had not received any formal medical training, John Hunter gained a distinguished reputation as an anatomist after following his brother William to London.

In common with his brother he was an avid collector, and his collection of medical specimens and artefacts are contained in the Hunterian Museum housed at the Royal College of Surgeons, in London.

While the Hunters have been recognised for their distinguished contributions both as soldiers and men of medicine, their motto, crest, coat of arms, and tartan all recall their origins as hunters.

The motto boldly declares 'I accomplish the hunt', while the crest features a greyhound. The coat of arms, fittingly, proudly displays three hunting horns.

Up until 1983 three separate tartans were associated with the family. One was a tartan shared with the Galbraith, Mitchell, and Russell families, one was known as the Hunters of Bute tartan and another as the Hunters of Peebles-shire tartan.

Neil Hunter, the 29th Laird of Hunterston and Clan Chief, resolved that the family should have its own tartan, and commissioned the creation of a new sett.

Known as the Hunterston Sett, or the Clan Hunter tartan, it features a green hunting ground colour, while a yellow stripe recalls the family's ancient roots as huntsmen to the king.

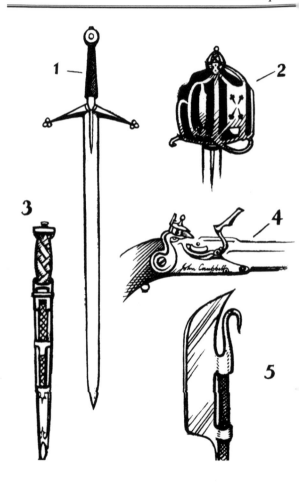

Clan weapons

1) The claymore or two-handed sword
   (fifteenth or early sixteenth century)

2) Basket hilt of broadsword
   made in Stirling, 1716

3) Highland dirk
   (eighteenth century)

4) Steel pistol *(detail)* made in Doune

5) Head of Lochaber Axe as carried
   in the '45 and earlier